NÜ METAL

HLE

Hal Leonard Europe
Distributed by Music Sales

RECORDED VERSIONS GUITAR

AUTHENTIC TRANSCRIPTIONS
WITH NOTES AND TABLATURE

CW00741027

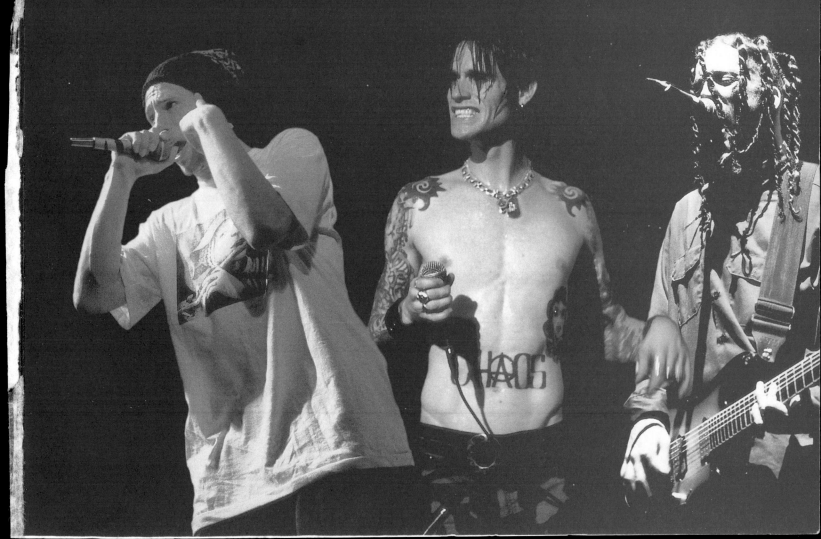

Exclusive Distributors:

Music Sales Limited

8/9 Frith Street, London W1D 3JB, England.

Music Sales Pty Limited

120 Rothschild Avenue, Rosebery, NSW 2018, Australia.

Order No. HLE90001531

ISBN 0-7119-8733-5

This book © Copyright 2001 by Hal Leonard Europe.

Cover design by Phil Gambrill.

Cover photographs courtesy of LFI.

Printed in the USA.

Your Guarantee of Quality:

As publishers, we strive to produce every book

to the highest commercial standards.

The book has been carefully designed to minimise awkward

page turns and to make playing from it a real pleasure.

Throughout, the printing and binding have been planned to ensure

a sturdy, attractive publication which should give years of enjoyment.

If your copy fails to meet our high standards, please inform us

and we will gladly replace it.

Music Sales' complete catalogue describes thousands of titles and is

available in full colour sections by subject, direct from Music Sales Limited.

Please state your areas of interest and send a cheque/postal order

for £1.50 for postage to:

Music Sales Limited, Newmarket Road, Bury St. Edmunds,

Suffolk IP33 3YB, England.

www.musicsales.com

Black

Words and Music by Sevendust

Lyrics:
1. Voices call, they call out my name,
3. Shadows follow so close behind me.

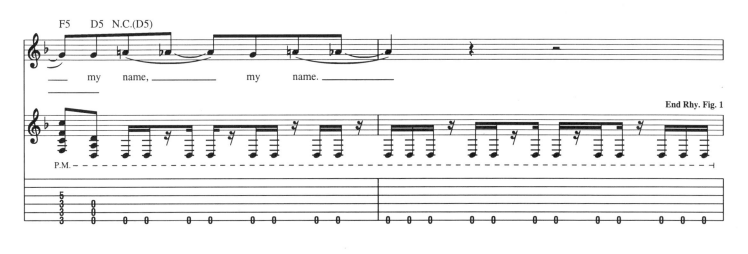

F5 D5 N.C.(D5)

_____ my name, _____ my name. _____

End Rhy. Fig. 1

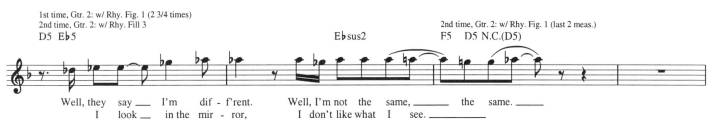

1st time, Gtr. 2: w/ Rhy. Fig. 1 (2 3/4 times)
2nd time, Gtr. 2: w/ Rhy. Fill 3

D5 Eb5

2nd time, Gtr. 2: w/ Rhy. Fig. 1 (last 2 meas.)

Ebsus2   F5   D5 N.C.(D5)

Well, they say _____ I'm dif - f'rent. Well, I'm not the same, _____ the same. _____
I look _____ in the mir - ror, I don't like what I see. _____

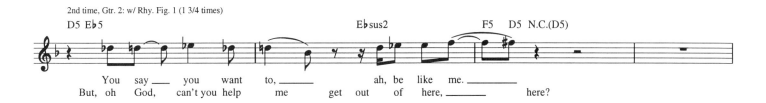

2nd time, Gtr. 2: w/ Rhy. Fig. 1 (1 3/4 times)

D5 Eb5   Ebsus2   F5   D5 N.C.(D5)

You say _____ you want to, _____ ah, be like me. _____
But, oh God, can't you help me get out of here, _____ here?

To Coda 1

D5 Eb5   Ebsus2   F5   D5 N.C.(D5)

Gtr. 2: w/ Rhy. Fill 1

Well, boy, _____ let me tell ya, you don't know what I seen. _____
Well, feel _____ like I'm liv - in' deep in hell. _____

N.C.

Gtr. 2
Riff B   End Riff B

P.M. ¬   P.M. P.M. P.M. P.M.   P.M. ¬   P.M. P.M. P.M.
Harm.   Harm. Harm. Harm. Harm.   Harm.   Harm. Harm. Harm.

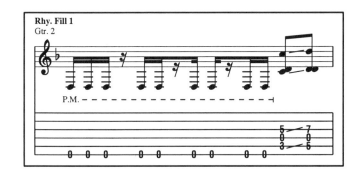

Rhy. Fill 1
Gtr. 2

P.M.

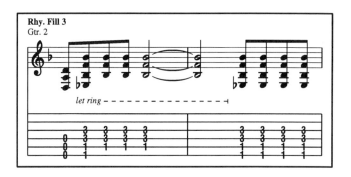

Rhy. Fill 3
Gtr. 2

let ring

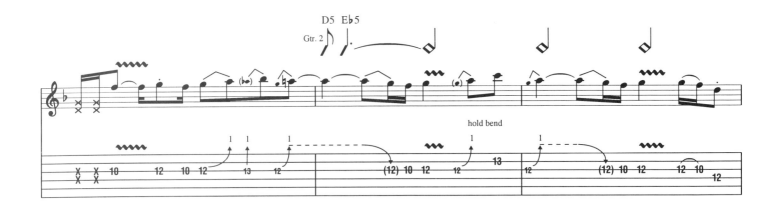

D.S.S. al Coda 3

Coda 3

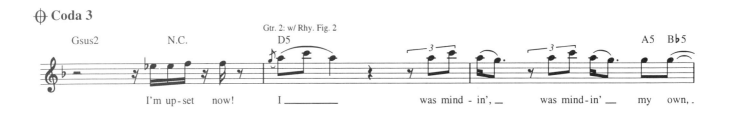

I'm up-set now! I _____ was mind-in', ___ was mind-in' ___ my own, ___

Outro

- own. _____ I ain't do-in' noth-in' wrong. _____ I ain't do-in' noth-

- in' wrong. _____ Well, noth-in' wrong. _____

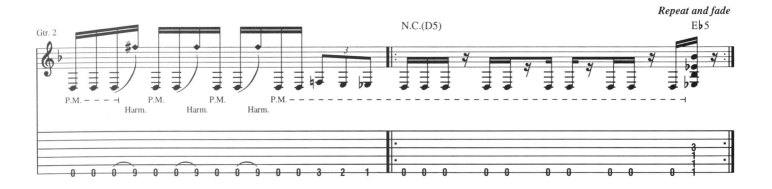

Bleed

Words by Max Cavalera and Fred Durst
Music by Max Cavalera

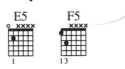

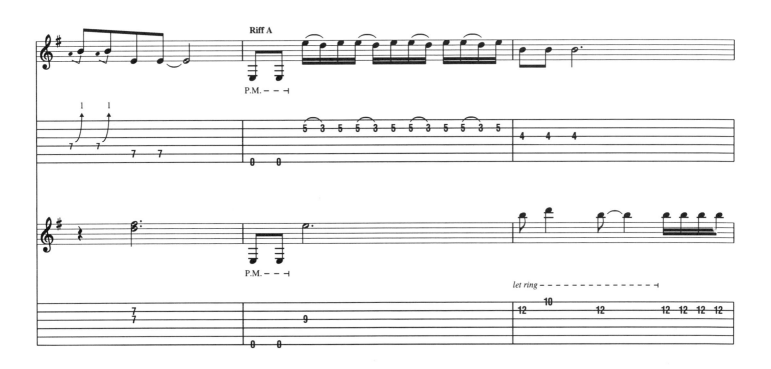

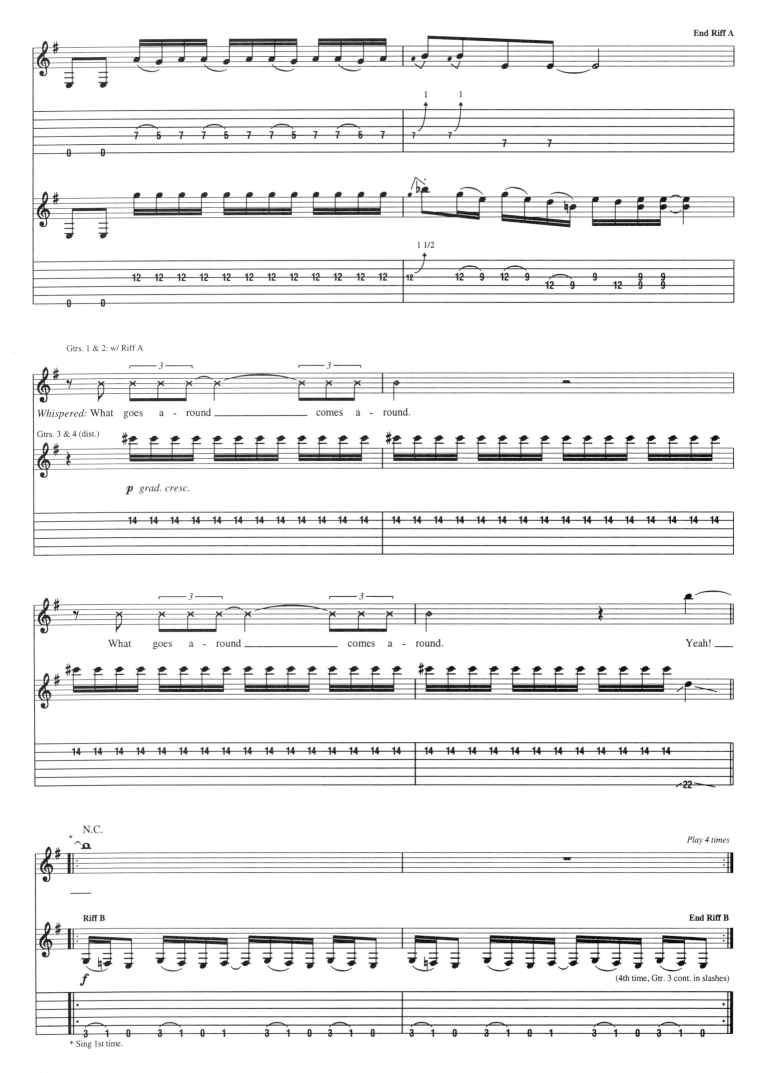

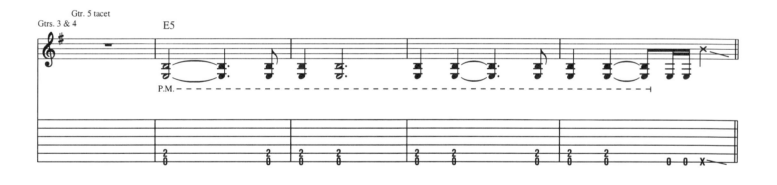

1. What goes a-round comes a-round. You bet-ter re-al-ize. You kill life, you kill life. Why? Why?
2. What goes a-round comes a-round. No more lies. You kill life, you kill life. Why? Why?

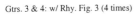

Gtrs. 3 & 4: w/ Rhy. Fig. 3 (4 times)

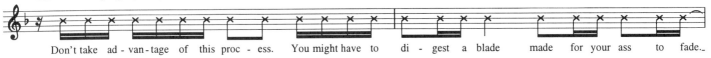

Don't take ad - van - tage of this proc - ess. You might have to di - gest a blade made for your ass to fade.

___ I'm liv - in' on in - stinct, nev - er think when I'm rush - in', bones ___ crush - in'. When I

put your sor - ry ass in a pack - age, you piece of ___ shit, sealed and de - liv - ered from a ___ sav - age.

And now you sweat be - cause you're go - in' down, you en - vi - ous clown. Fuck - in'

A Tempo

F5

Gtr. 3

Gtr. 3 tacet

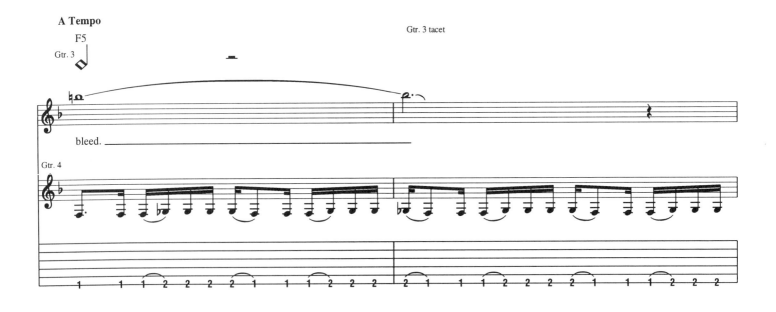

bleed. _____

Gtr. 4

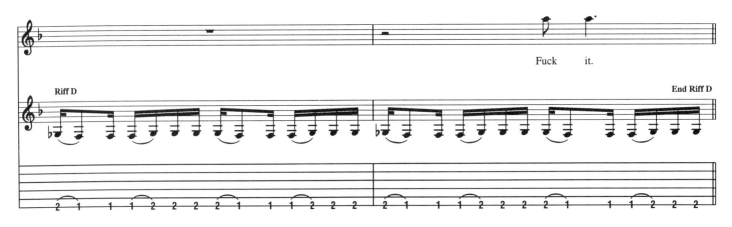

Fuck it.

Riff D

End Riff D

Bulls on Parade

Music Written and Arranged by Rage Against The Machine
Lyrics by Zack De La Rocha

Guitar Solo

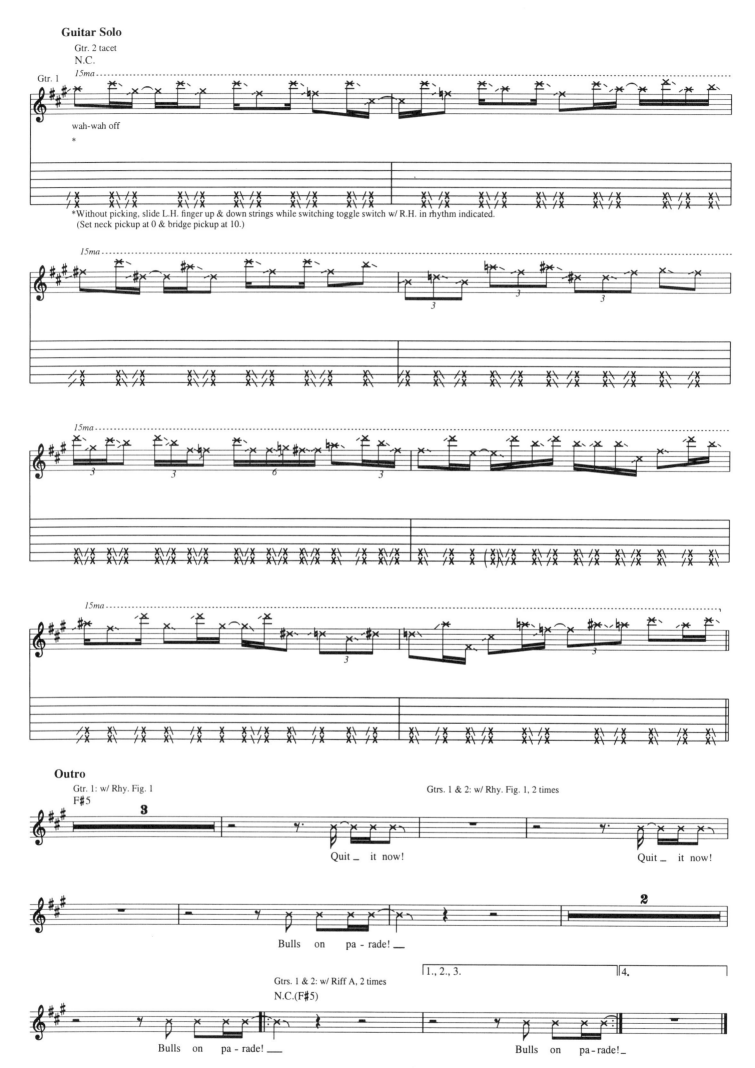

Outro

Come Original

Music by Nicholas Hexum and Aaron Wills
Lyrics by Nicholas Hexum and Doug Martinez

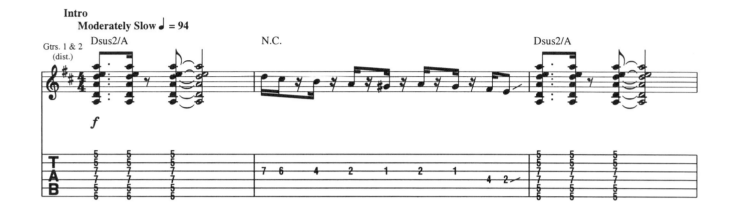

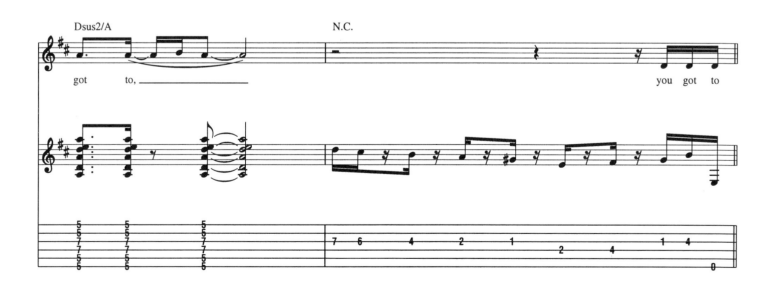

Chorus

come o - rig - i - nal, you got to come o - rig - i - nal. All en - ter - tain - ers, come o - rig - i - nal. You got to

Gtrs. 1 & 2: w/ Rhy. Fig. 1

come o - rig - i - nal, you got to come o - rig - i - nal. All en - ter - tain - ers, hear why. 1. To

Verse

Gtrs. 1 & 2: w/ Rhy. Fig. 1, 2 times

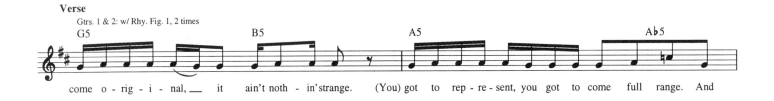

come o - rig - i - nal, __ it ain't noth - in' strange. (You) got to rep - re - sent, you got to come full range. And

full range of e - mo - tion, full range of styles. When you come to town you'll have them com - in' for miles. And

Chorus

Gtrs. 1 & 2: w/ Rhy. Fig. 1, 2 times

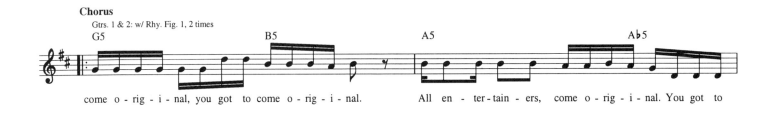

come o - rig - i - nal, you got to come o - rig - i - nal. All en - ter - tain - ers, come o - rig - i - nal. You got to

come o - rig - i - nal, you got to come o - rig - i - nal. All en - ter - tain - ers, hear why.

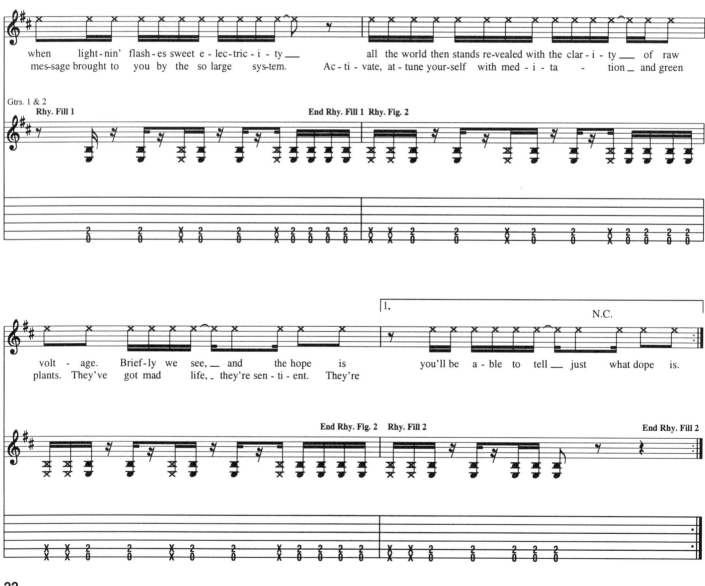

Some of them whine and some them bitch. They can-not do it, nev-er switch. Com-in' up from the heart _ and de-liv-ered with a wild _ pitch.

Gtrs. 1 & 2: w/ Rhy. Fill 2

Sit up on top of the rhy-thm like a wild _ stal-li-on. This is the rul-ing sys-tem.

Interlude

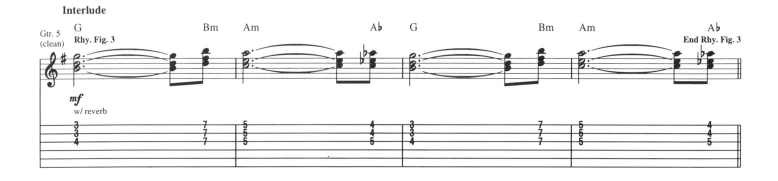

Gtr. 5
(clean)

Rhy. Fig. 3

G | Bm Am | A♭ G | Bm Am | A♭

End Rhy. Fig. 3

mf
w/ reverb

Outro-Chorus

Gtrs. 1 & 2: w/ Rhy. Fig. 1
Gtr. 5: w/ Rhy. Fig. 3

G | Bm Am | A♭

1., 2., 3.

Come o-rig-i-nal, you got to come o-rig-i-nal. All en-ter-tain-ers, come o-rig-i-nal. You got to

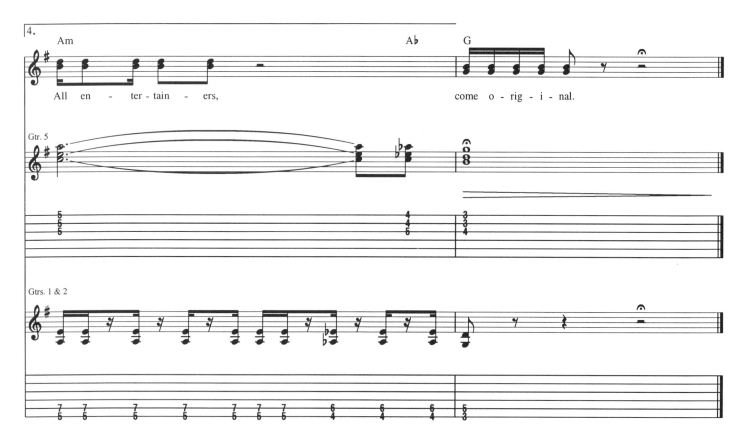

4.

Am | A♭ G

All en-ter-tain-ers, come o-rig-i-nal.

Gtr. 5

Gtrs. 1 & 2

Flowing

Music and Lyrics by Nicholas Hexum

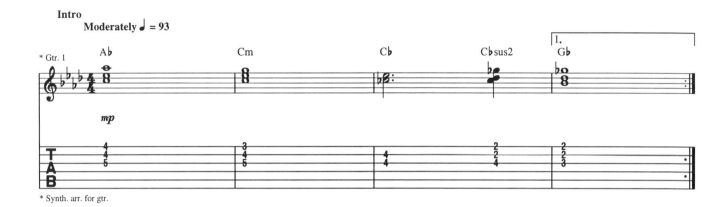

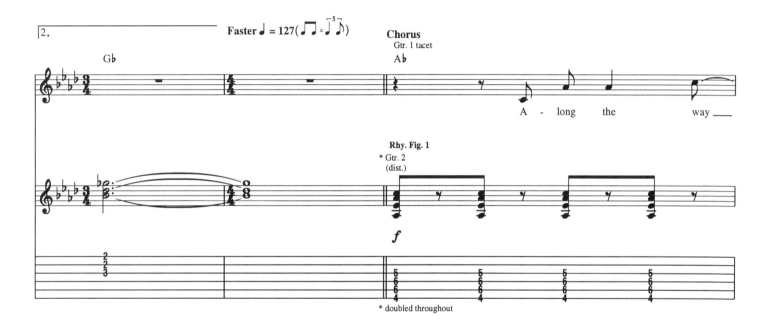

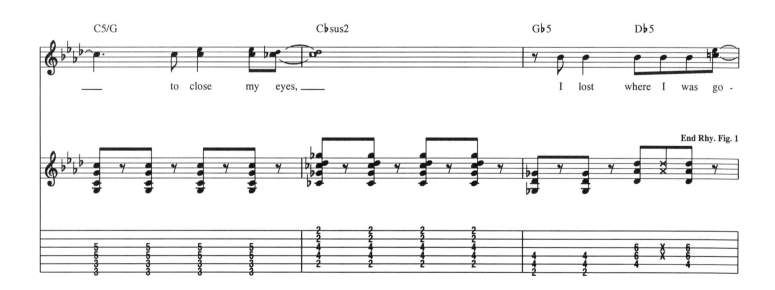

pect to lay a-wake there by _____ your sleep - ing girl. _____
end - less - ly re - play - ing times that were _____ un - kind. _____

If some - bod - y cares _____ then there _____ is no way you can tell. _____
Go a - way, sun, _____ I'm not pre - pared _____ for you to -

Gtr. 2

P.M.

To Coda 1

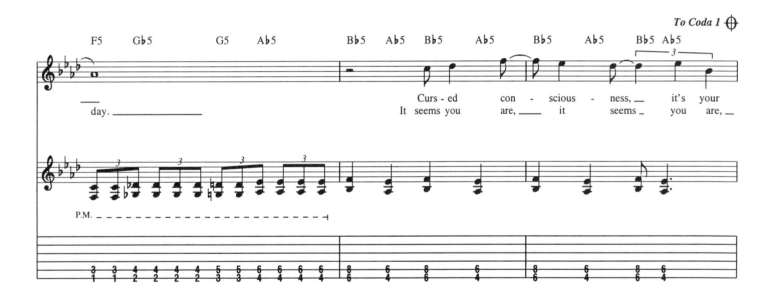

_____ Curs - ed con - scious - ness, _____ it's your
day. _____ It seems you are, _____ it seems _____ you are, _____

P.M.

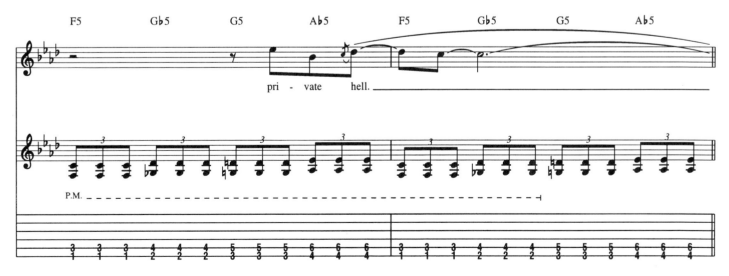

pri - vate hell. _____

P.M.

27

Guerrilla Radio

Written and Arranged by Rage Against The Machine

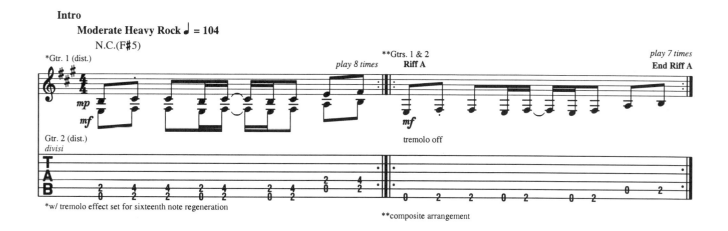

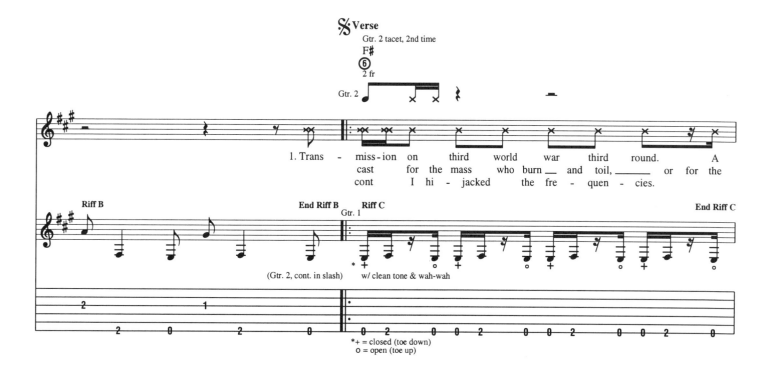

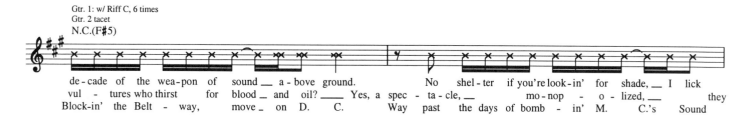

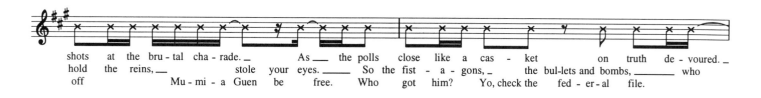

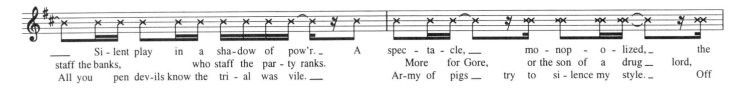

_____ Si - lent play in a sha-dow of pow'r. _____ A
staff the banks, who staff the par - ty ranks.
All you pen dev-ils know the tri - al was vile. _____

1.

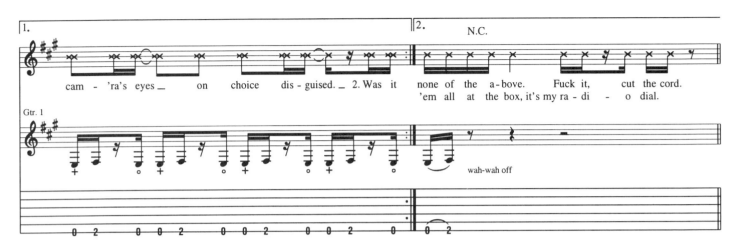

cam - 'ra's eyes _____ on choice dis - guised. _____ 2. Was it

2. N.C.

none of the a - bove. Fuck it, cut the cord.
'em all at the box, it's my ra - di - o dial.

Gtr. 1

wah-wah off

Chorus

Gtrs. 1 & 2: w/ Riff A, 7 times

N.C.(F#5)

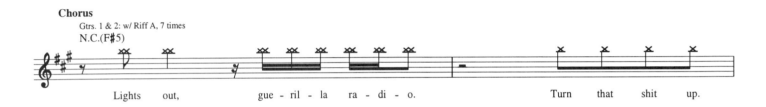

Lights out, gue - ril - la ra - di - o. Turn that shit up.

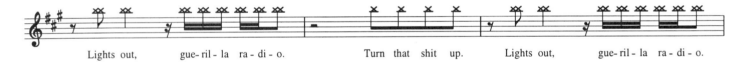

Lights out, gue - ril - la ra - di - o. Turn that shit up. Lights out, gue - ril - la ra - di - o.

To Coda ⊕

D.S. al Coda
(take 2nd ending)

Gtrs. 1 & 2: w/ Riff B

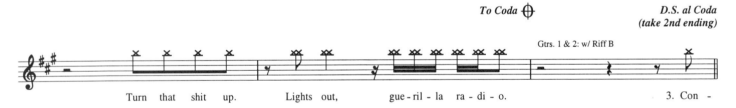

Turn that shit up. Lights out, gue - ril - la ra - di - o. 3. Con -

⊕ *Coda*

Interlude

Gtr. 1: w/ Riff A

* Gtr. 1: w/ Riff A, 8 times
Gtr. 2 tacet

Gtr. 2: w/ Riff A, 4 times

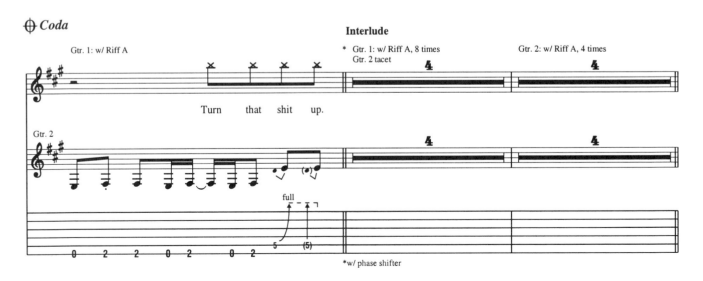

Turn that shit up.

Gtr. 2

full

*w/ phase shifter

30

Guitar Solo

Gtr. 1 N.C.(F#5)

f

Gtr. 3 (dist.)
divisi *w/ Digitech Whammy Pedal & talk box

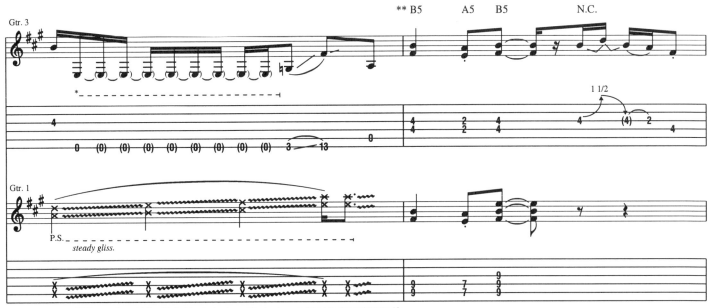

*set for two octaves above

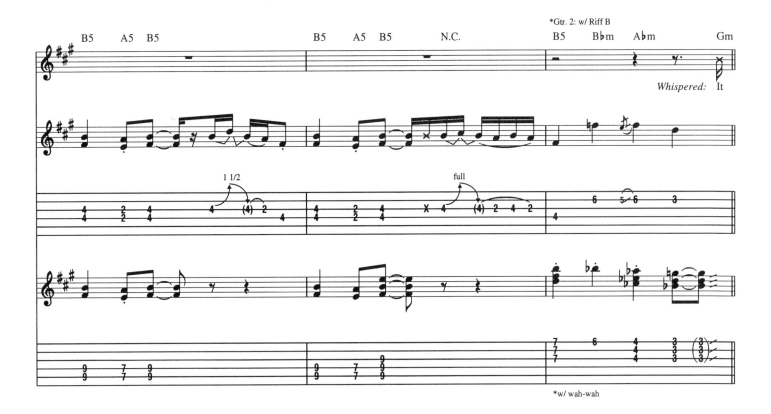

*Using a guitar with Les Paul style electronics, set lead volume to 0 and rhythm volume to 10.
Strike the strings while the pickup selector swtich is the lead position, then flip the switch to
the rhythm position to simulate the attack. Flip switch in specified rhythm.   **Chord symbols reflect basic tonality.

Whispered: It

*Gtr. 2: w/ Riff B

*w/ wah-wah

Outro

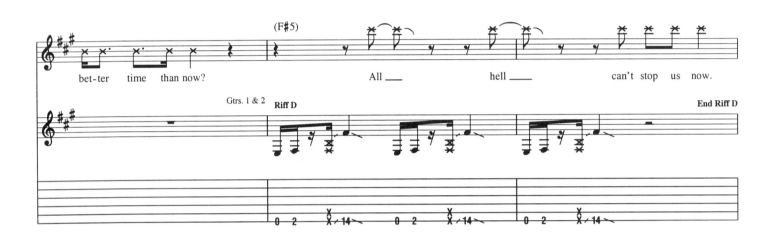

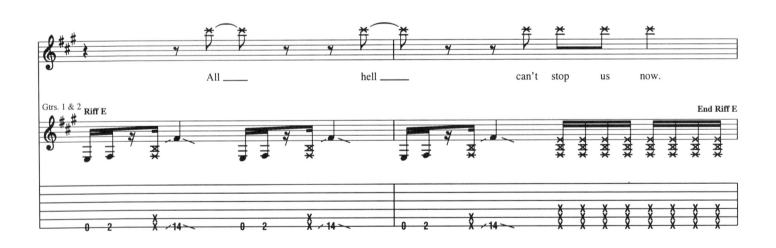

32

Just Like This

Words and Music by Fred Durst, Wes Borland, John Otto and Sam River

Tune Down 1½ Step:
① = C♯ ④ = B
② = G♯ ⑤ = F♯
③ = E   ⑥ = C♯

Intro

Moderate Rock ♩ = 102

N.C.

*Get up.   Get up.   Ah, like

*w/echo repeats

2.

Gtr. 1: w/Riff A1

G5   G#5   N.C.   G5   G#5

- in' at me.___ And I do___ what it takes,___ if I make___ some mis-takes___ it's o-kay___

Bridge
Gtr. 1 tacet

G5   G#5   N.C.(C#5)

___ 'cause it's all___ just the way___ it should be.___   *Ah, break it.   Limp
                                                          *w/echo repeats

(Bm)   (C#5)   (Bm)   (Bsus4)

Biz - kit's in the house,___ y'all.

(C#5)   (Bm)

                                         Limp Biz - kit's in the house,___ y'all.

Gtr. 1

*

*Bounce edge of pick on the high E string over pickups.

(C#5)   (Bm)   (Bsus4)

(C#5)   (Bm)

                                         Limp Biz - kit's in the house,___ y'all.

Last Resort

Words and Music by Papa Roach

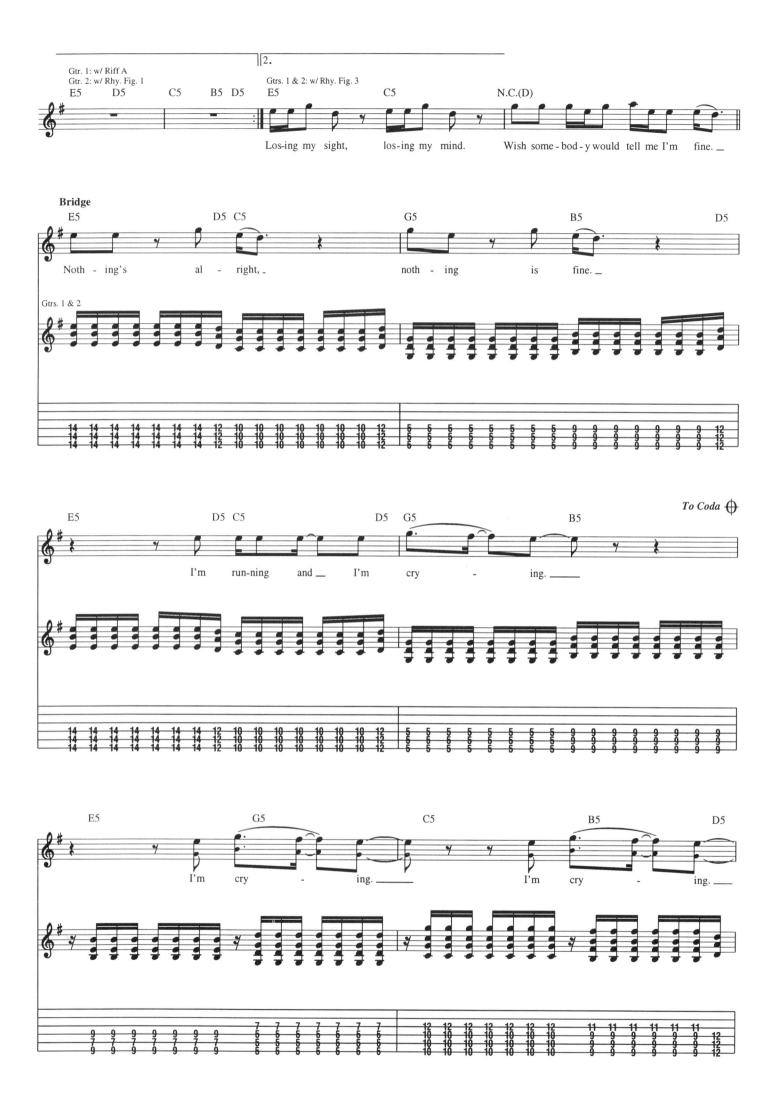

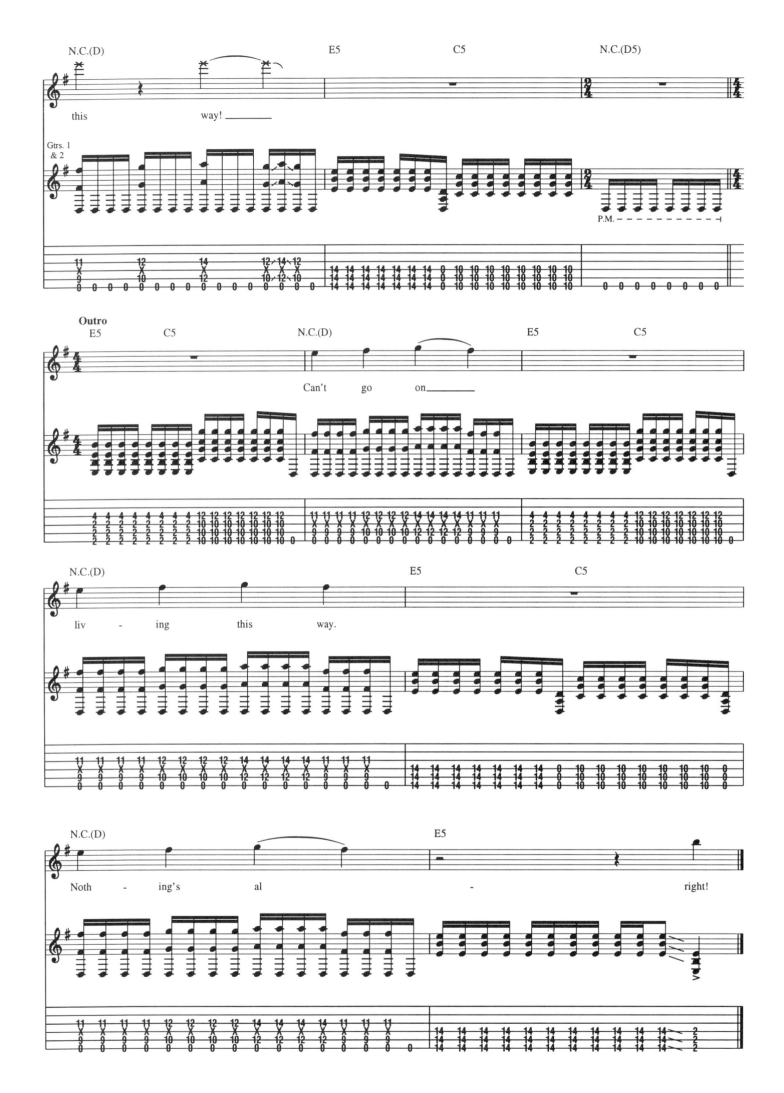

Lit Up

Words and Music by Joshua Todd Gruber, Keith Edward Nelson, Jonathan Brightman and Devon Glenn

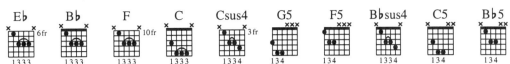

*Key signature denotes G Mixolydian.

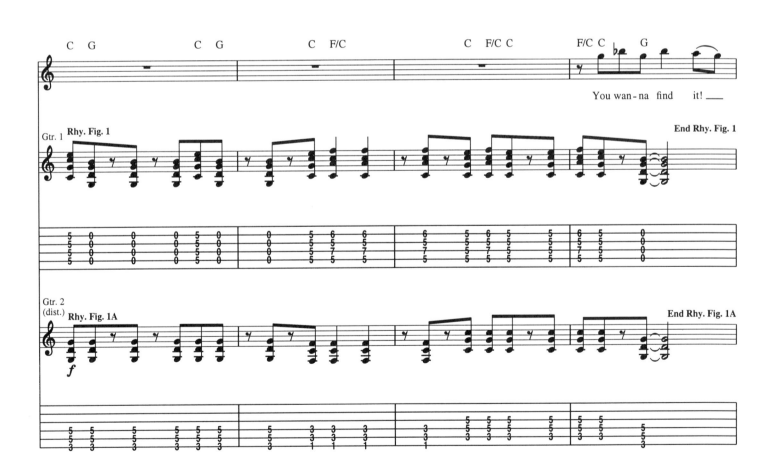

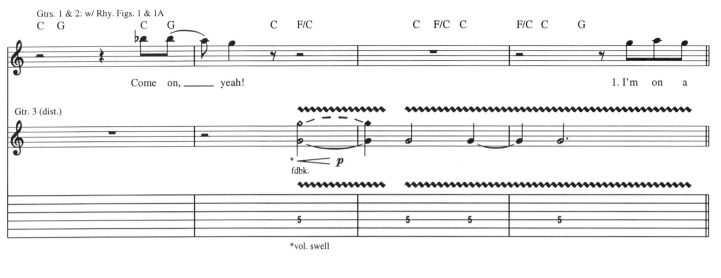

Gtrs. 1 & 2: w/ Rhy. Figs. 1 & 1A

C G   C G   C F/C   C F/C C   F/C C G

Come on, _____ yeah!   1. I'm on a

Gtr. 3 (dist.)

*vol. swell

Verse

Gtrs. 1 & 2: w/ Rhy. Figs. 1 & 1A, 2 times
Gtr. 3 tacet

C G   C G   C F/C   C F/C C   F/C C G

plane   with co - caine _____   and, yes, I'm all lit up a - gain. _____   Cup of _____
train   and right on, _____   you know the train is stay-in' off the track. _____   I'm in touch, _

C G   C G   C F/C   C F/C C   F/C C G

_____ love _____   and touch-in'. _____   Your ma - ma said pack-in' lines _ a sin. _____   }
_____ love, _____   from this crutch. _   When you're in tempt of mon-ey I'm on e - lev - en. }   And, yes, I'm

𝄋 Chorus

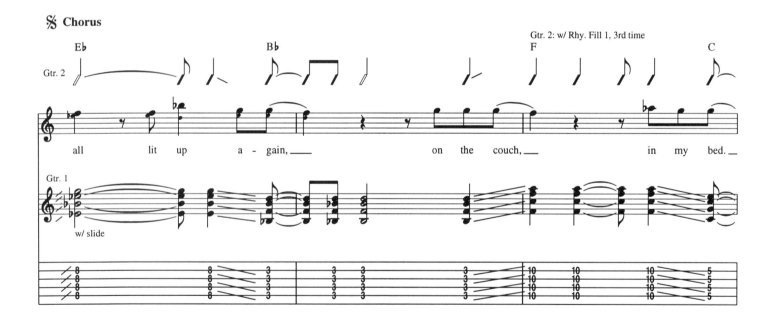

Eb   Bb   F   C

Gtr. 2: w/ Rhy. Fill 1, 3rd time

Gtr. 2

all   lit up a - gain, _____   on the couch, _____   in my bed. _____

Gtr. 1

w/ slide

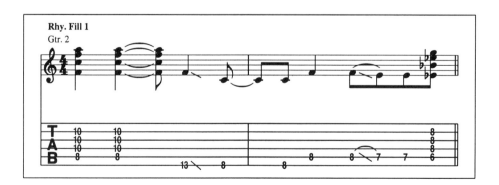

Rhy. Fill 1
Gtr. 2

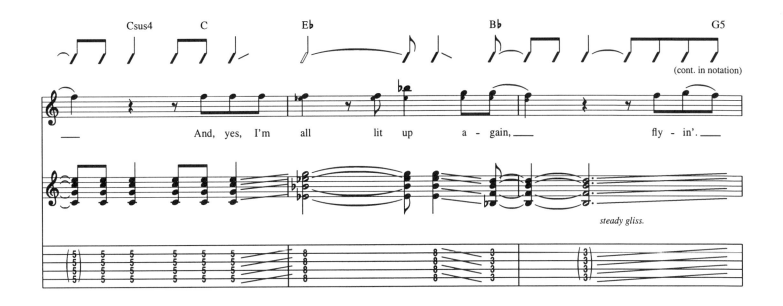

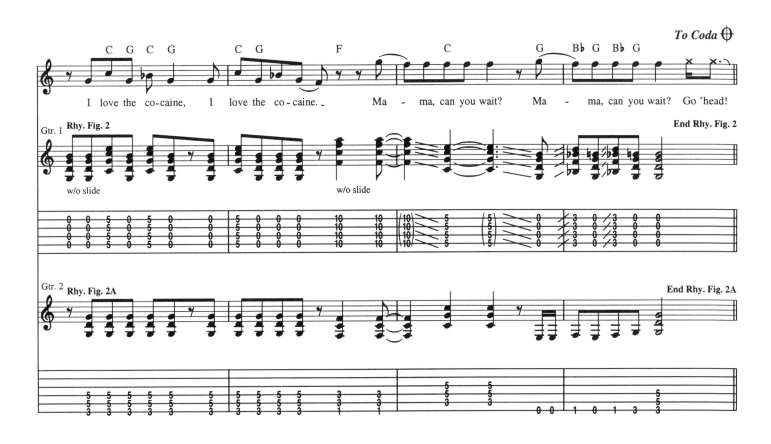

I love the co-caine, I love the co-caine. Ma - ma, can you wait? Oh, can you wait long?

Guitar Solo

Bridge

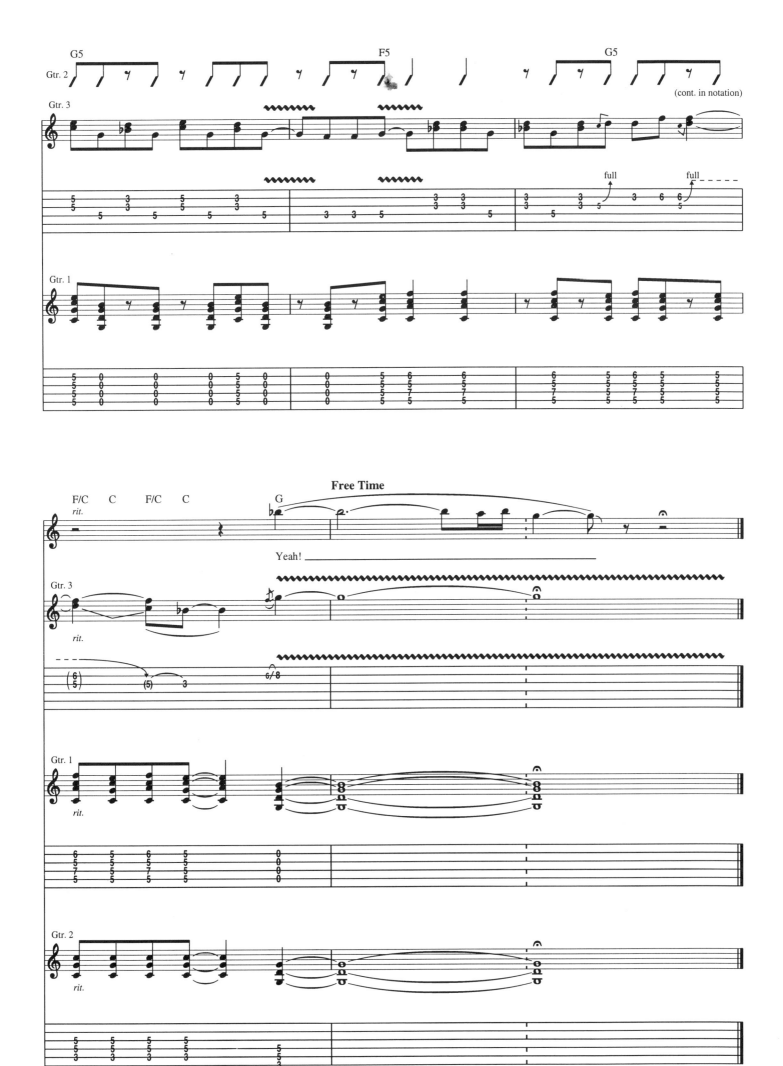

Loco

Words by B. Dez Fafara
Music by Miguel Rascon, Rayna Foss and Mike Cox

through the sys - tem, out __ to the right. Said, "You're in my light, _____ uh."

Lock down the gen - er - a - tor on, man. Screw down, use the sys - tem, use the main plan.

Full pow - er up __ to the point man. _____ Don't fuck _____ with me.

Chorus
C#

Lo - co, lo - co, lo - co,

Gtrs. 3 & 4

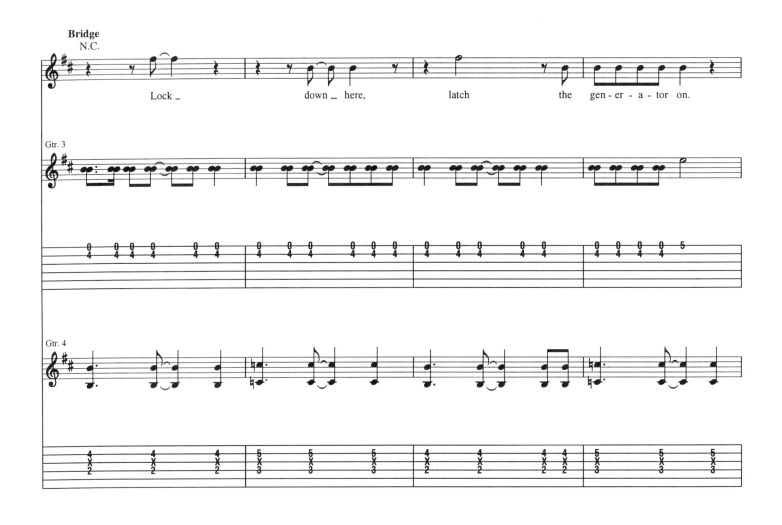

Spoken: Steamroller rollin' through my head, said attached to loco. Power up coal to the system, out to the right. Said, "You're in my light."

55

Make Me Bad

Words and Music by Reginald Arvizu, Jonathan Davis, James Shaffer, David Silveria and Brian Welch

7-String Gtrs.;
Tune Down 1 Step:
①=D ④=C
②=A ⑤=G
③=F ⑥=D
⑦=A

*Set to produce notes one octave above fretted pitch.

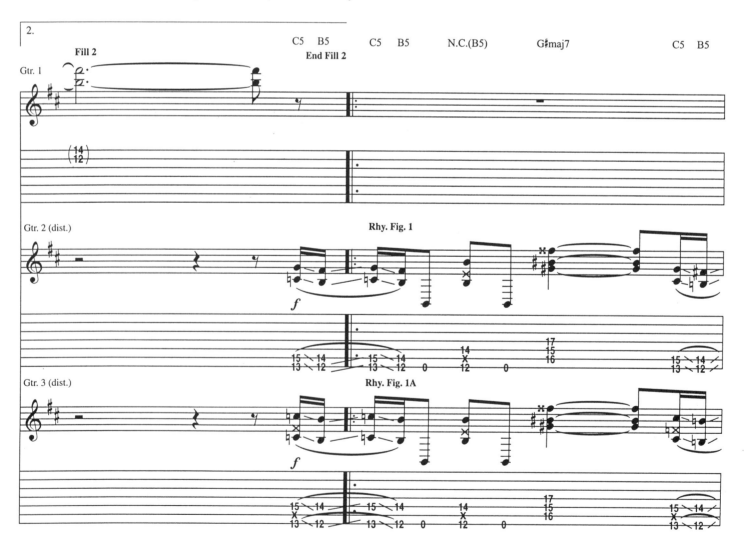

I feel the rea - son as___ it's leav - ing me.___ No, not___ a- gain.___

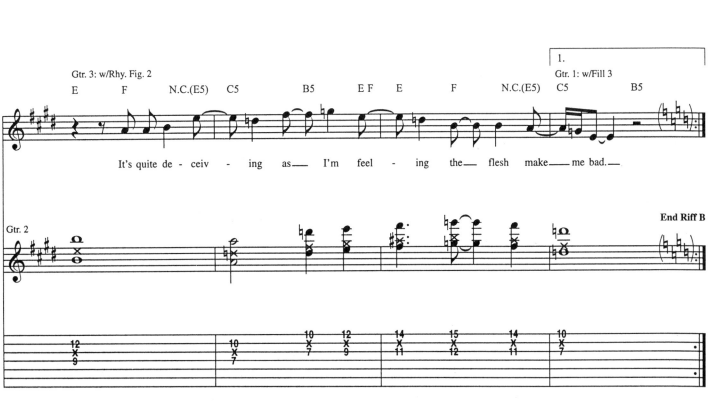

It's quite de- ceiv - ing as___ I'm feel - ing the flesh make___ me bad.___

Additional Lyrics

2. All I do is look for you.
   I need my fix, you need it too,
   Just to get some sort of attention, attention.
   What does it mean to you? (What does it mean to you?)
   For me, it's something I just do. (I just do.)
   I want something, I need to feel the sickness in you.

Nobody's Real

Lyrics by Spider. Music by Powerman 5000

Gtrs. 1, 2 & 3: Tune down 1/2 step:
(low to high) Eb–Ab–Db–Gb–Bb–Eb

Gtr. 4: Drop D tuning, down 1/2 step:
(low to high) Db–Ab–Db–Gb–Bb–Eb

Intro

Moderate Rock ♩ = 124

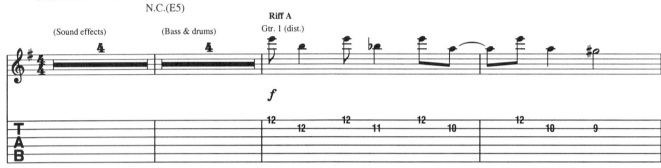

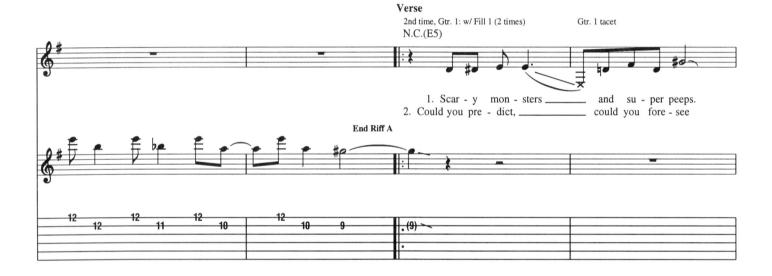

1. Scar - y mon - sters _____ and su - per peeps.
2. Could you pre - dict, _____ could you fore - see

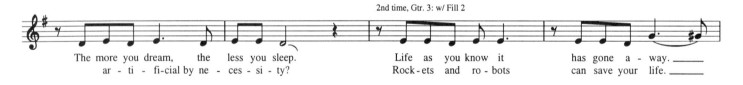

The more you dream, the less you sleep.
ar - ti - fi - cial by ne - ces - si - ty?

Life as you know it has gone a - way. _____
Rock - ets and ro - bots can save your life. _____

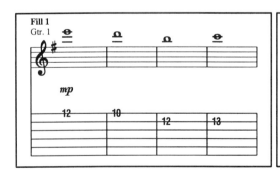

* Substitute a half rest for beats 3 & 4 of last meas.

** w/ heavy fuzz

Promise

Written by Max Collins, Jon Siebels and Tony Fagenson

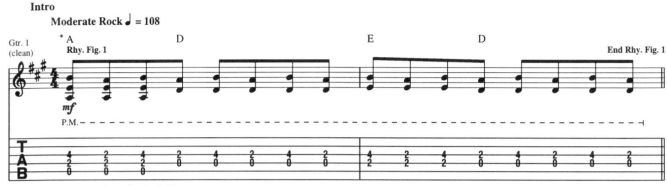

* Chord symbols reflect implied harmony.

Verse

1. Sleep - ing through the eve - ning, sing - ing dreams in - side my head. I'm head - ing out, I've got some ins who say they

care, and they just might. I run a - way with you if things don't go as planned. Plan - ning big could be a

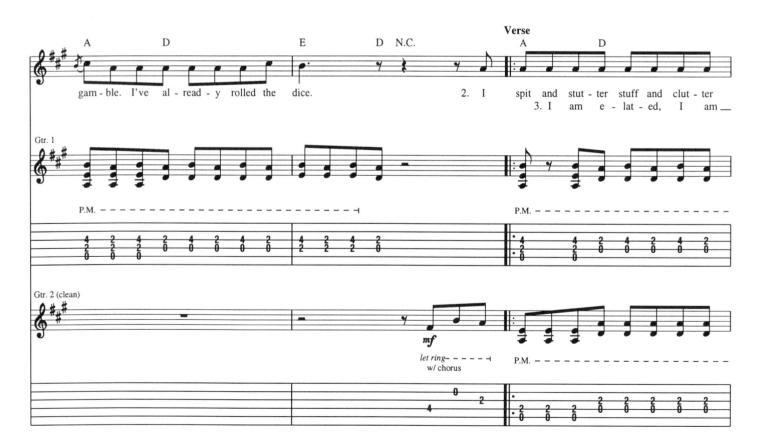

gam - ble. I've al - read - y rolled the dice.
2. I spit and stut - ter stuff and clut - ter
3. I am e - lat - ed, I am

wor - ries in my wor - ried cor - ner. Mal-ad-just - ed, just un - trust - ed, rust - ed, some-times bril - liant bust - ed
___ all smiles and dat - ed in my ___ man bites dog town with a Span - ish name.

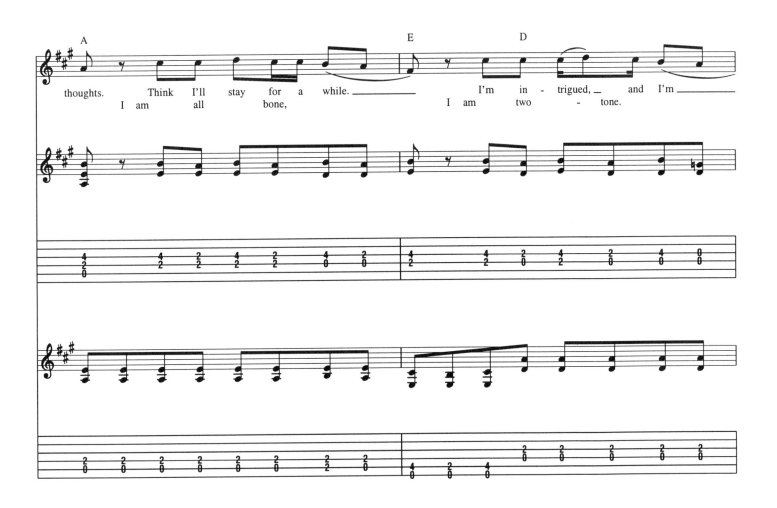

thoughts. Think I'll stay for a while. ___ I'm in - trigued, ___ and I'm ___
I am all bone, I am two - tone.

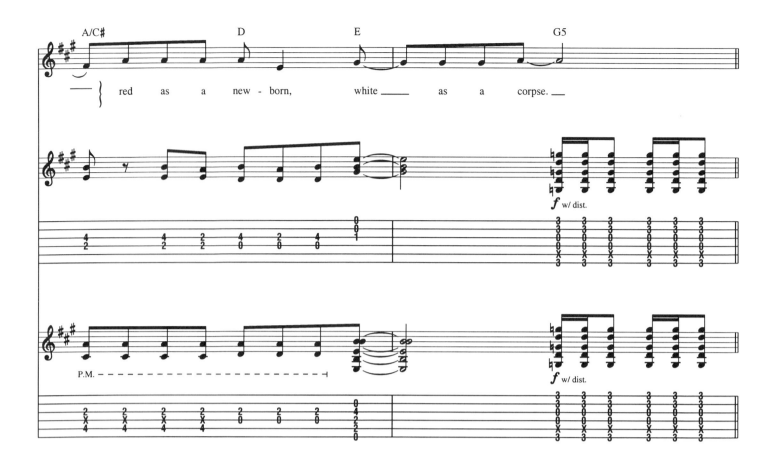

red as a new-born, white _____ as a corpse. _____

𝄉 Chorus

3rd time, Gtr. 1 tacet
3rd time, Gtr. 2: w/ Riff C (3 times)
3rd time, Gtr. 3: w/ Fill 1

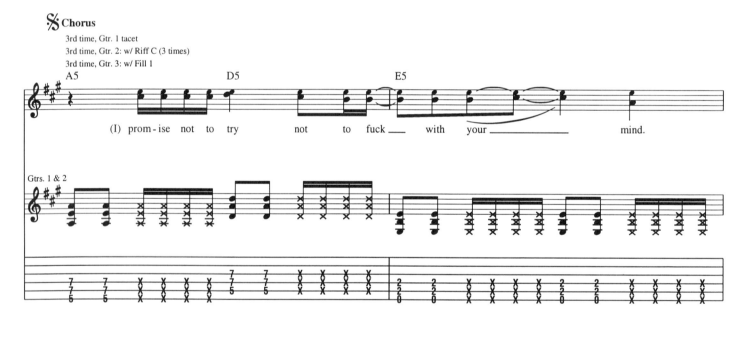

(I) prom-ise not to try   not   to fuck ___ with your _____ mind.

Gtrs. 1 & 2

Fill 1
Gtr. 3

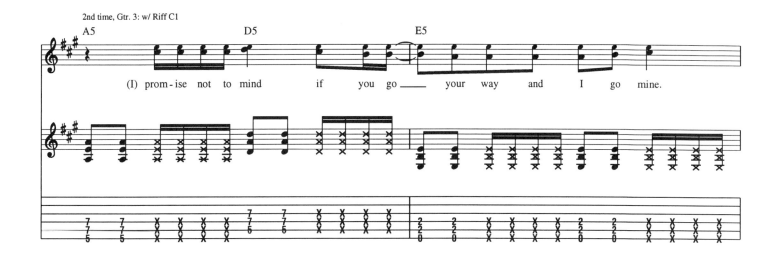

2nd time, Gtr. 3: w/ Riff C1

A5   D5   E5

(I) prom-ise not to mind   if   you   go _____ your way   and   I   go   mine.

To Coda ⊕

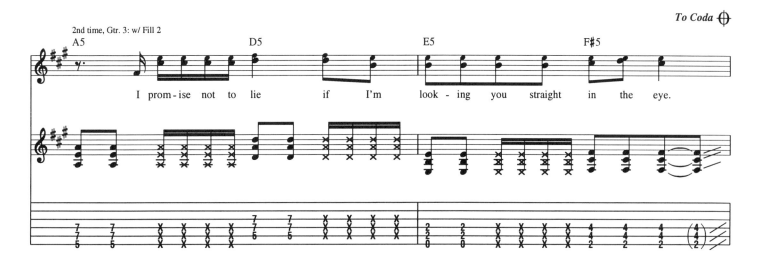

2nd time, Gtr. 3: w/ Fill 2

A5   D5   E5   F#5

I prom-ise not to lie   if   I'm   look-ing you straight in the eye.

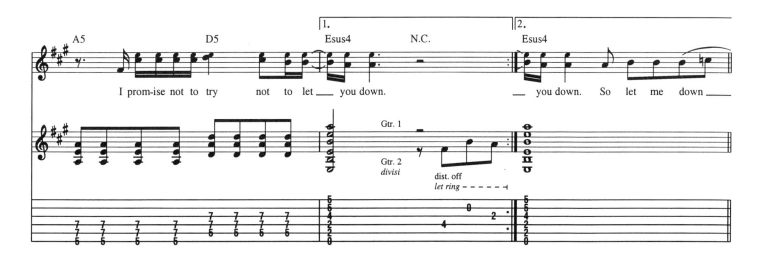

1.   2.

A5   D5   Esus4   N.C.   Esus4

I prom-ise not to try   not   to   let _____ you down.   _____ you down. So   let   me   down _____

Gtr. 1

Gtr. 2
divisi

dist. off
let ring - - - - - -

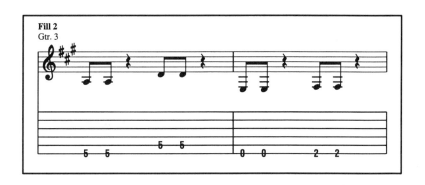

Fill 2
Gtr. 3

69

Interlude

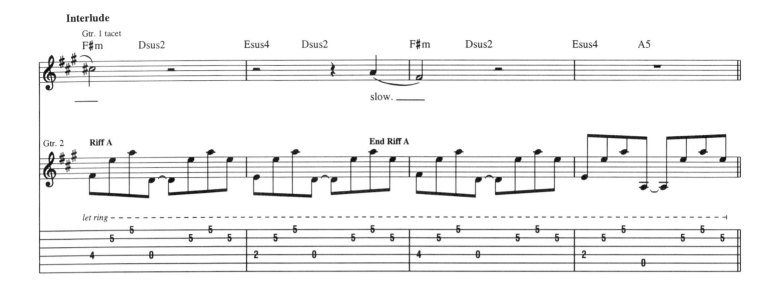

Bridge

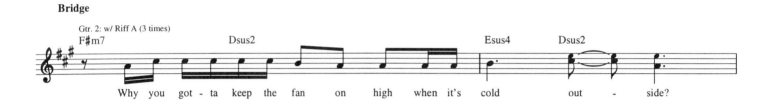

Why you got - ta keep the fan on high when it's cold out - side?

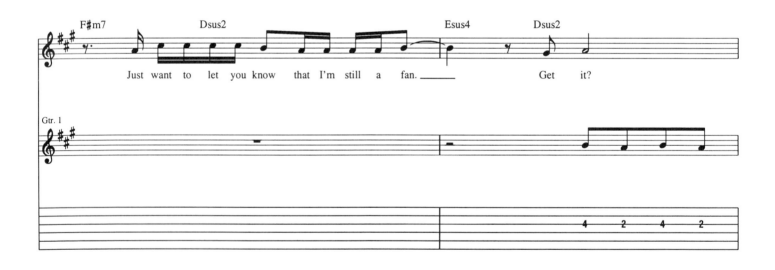

Just want to let you know that I'm still a fan. _____ Get it?

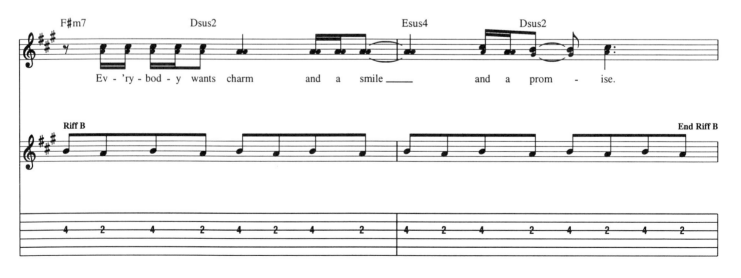

Ev - 'ry - bod - y wants charm and a smile _____ and a prom - ise.

Coda

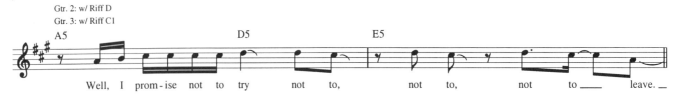

Well, I prom-ise not to try not to, not to, not to ___ leave. ___

Outro

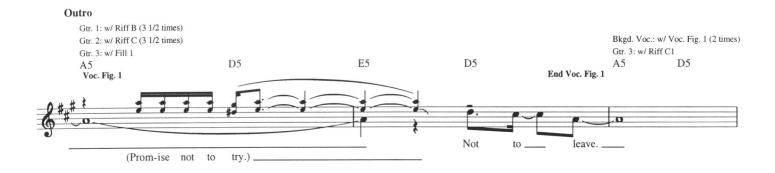

(Prom-ise not to try.) ___

Not to ___ leave. ___

Not to, not to ___ leave, ___ yeah. ___ I won't ___ leave, ___ I won't ___ leave. _

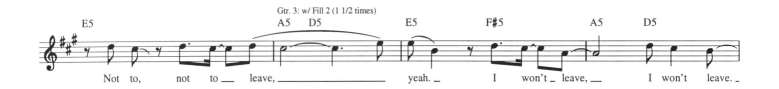

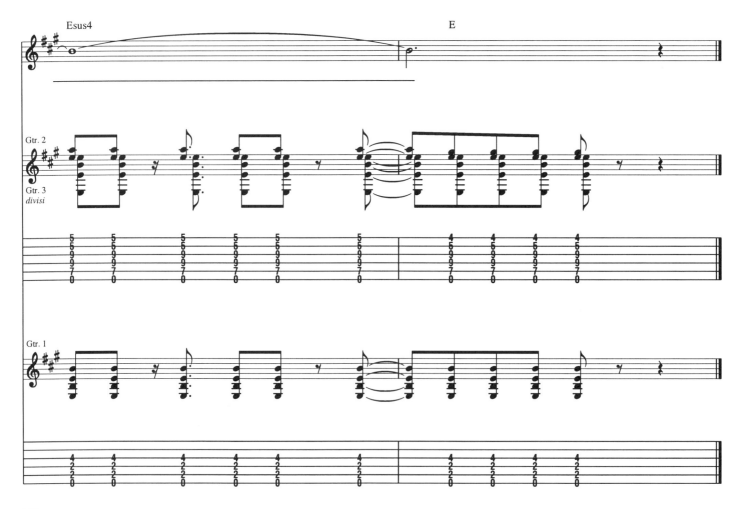

Spiders

Words and Music by Daron Malakian, Serj Tankian, Shavo Odadjian and John Dolmayan

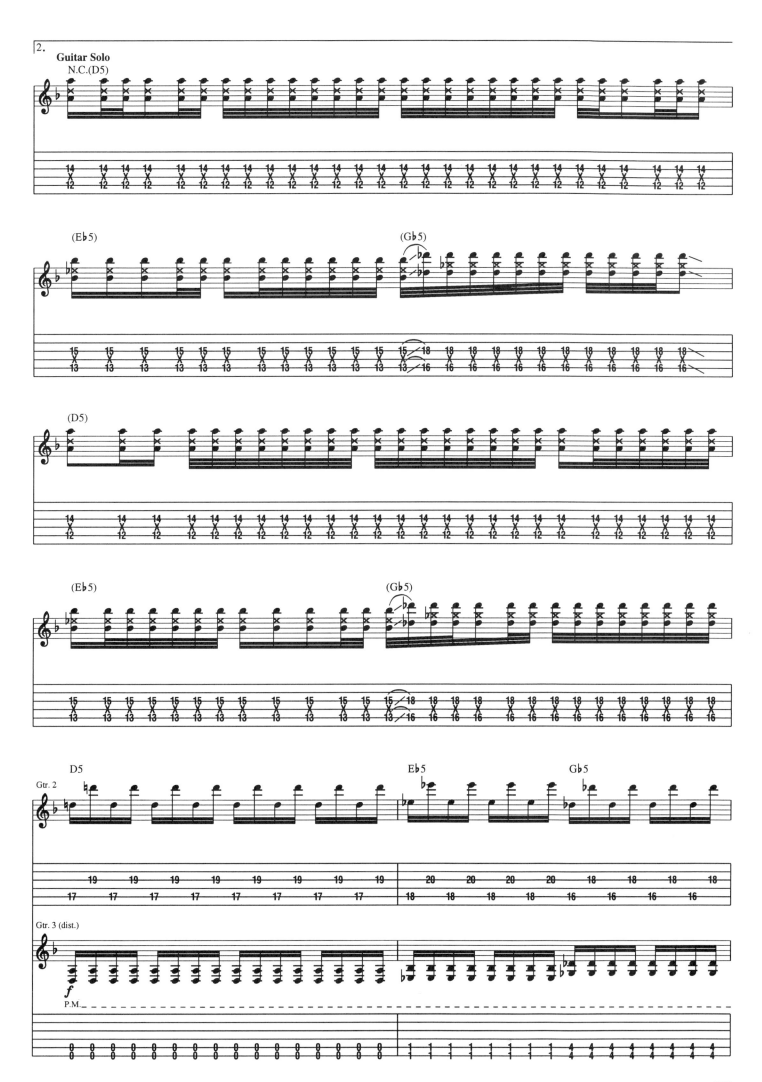

Sugar

Words and Music by Daron Malakian, Serj Tankian and Shavo Odadjian

sane.   Yeah, they call it in - sane.   I play Rus-sian rou-lette ev - 'ry day,   a

pock - et,   yeah,   right in my   pock - et.   My girl, you know she lash-es out at me some - times_

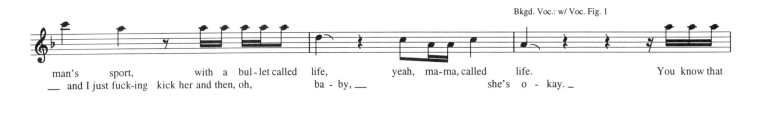

man's   sport,   with a bul - let called life,   yeah, ma-ma, called   life.   You know that

_ and I just fuck-ing kick her and then, oh,   ba - by, _   she's o - kay. _

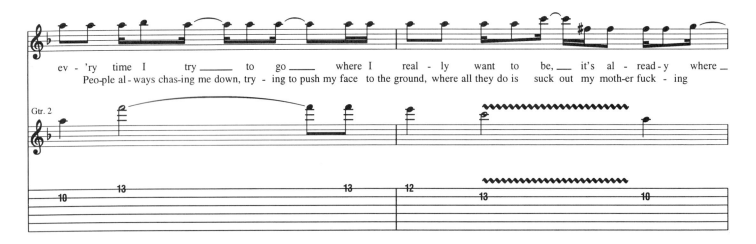

ev - 'ry time I   try _   to go _   where I real - ly   want to be, _ it's al - read - y where _

Peo-ple al - ways chas-ing me down, try - ing to push my face to the ground, where all they do is   suck out my moth-er fuck - ing

End Double-Time Feel

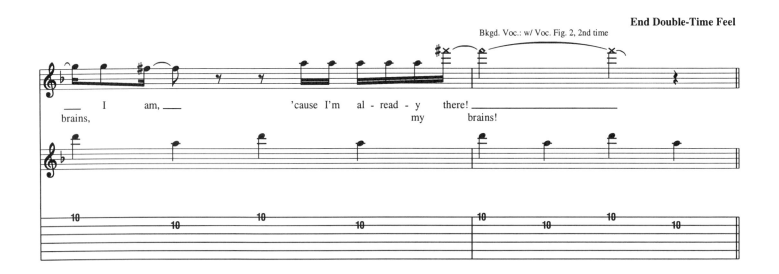

_   I   am, _   'cause I'm al - read - y   there! _____

brains,   my   brains!

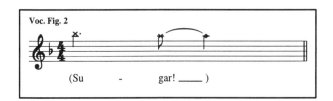

(Su - gar! _)

Outro

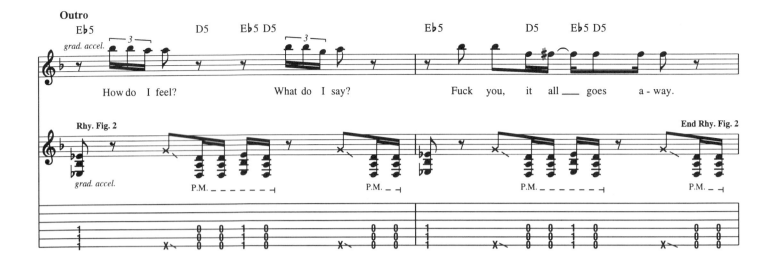

How do I feel? What do I say? Fuck you, it all ___ goes a - way.

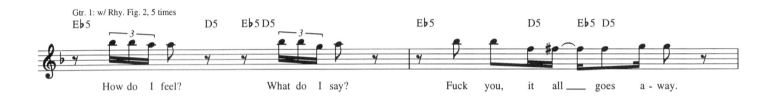

How do I feel? What do I say? Fuck you, it all ___ goes a - way.

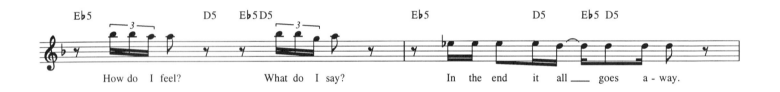

How do I feel? What do I say? In the end it all ___ goes a - way.

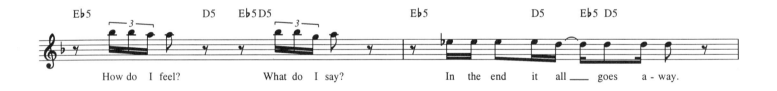

How do I feel? What do I say? In the end it all ___ goes a - way.

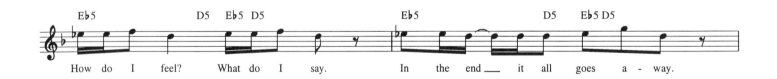

How do I feel? What do I say. In the end ___ it all goes a - way.

How do I feel? What do I say. In the end ___ it all goes a - way.

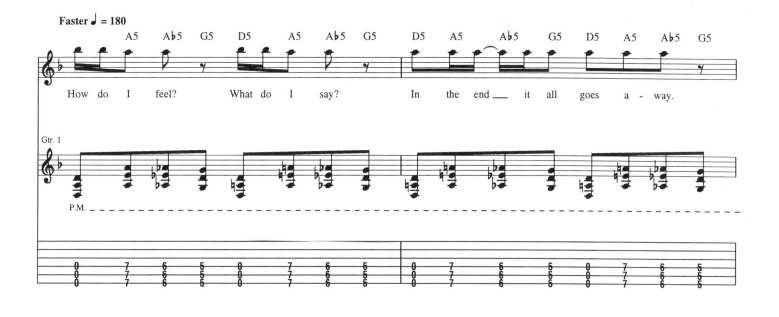

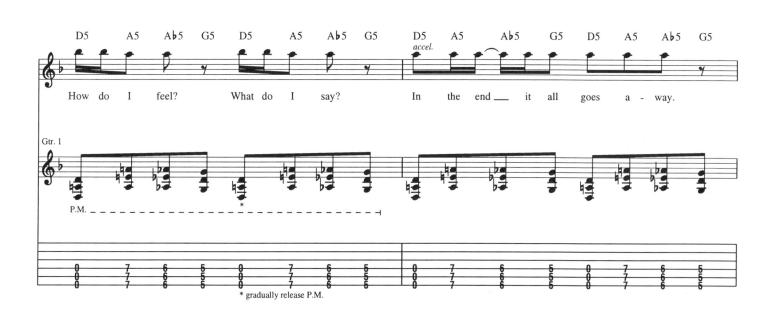

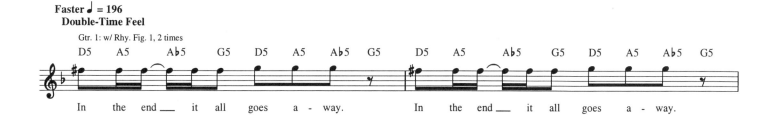

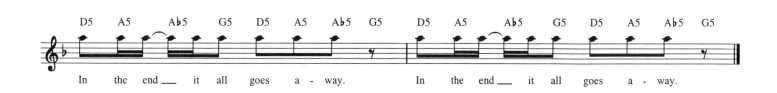

Take a Look Around
(Theme From "M:I-2")

from the Paramount Motion Picture M:I-2

Words and Music by Fred Durst and Lalo Schifrin

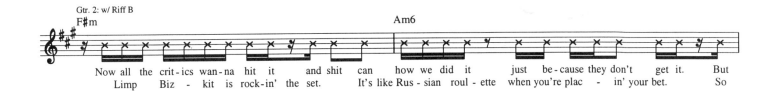

Gtr. 2: w/ Riff B

F#m   Am6

Now all the crit-ics wan-na hit it and shit can how we did it just be-cause they don't get it. But

Limp Biz - kit is rock-in' the set. It's like Rus - sian roul - ette when you're plac - in' your bet. So

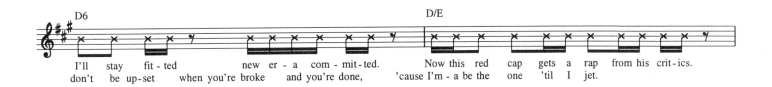

D6   D/E

I'll stay fit - ted new er - a com - mit-ted. Now this red cap gets a rap from his crit-ics.

don't be up-set when you're broke and you're done, 'cause I'm - a be the one 'til I jet.

1.

Gtr. 1: w/ Riff A

N.C.(F#m)   (A)

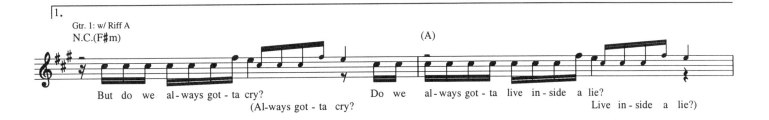

But do we al-ways got-ta cry?   Do we al-ways got-ta live in-side a lie?

(Al-ways got - ta cry?)   Live in - side a lie?)

(D)   (E)

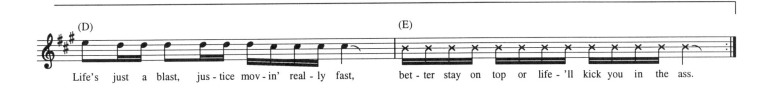

Life's just a blast, jus-tice mov-in' real-ly fast, better stay on top or life-'ll kick you in the ass.

2.

% **Chorus**

N.C.

I know why you wan - na hate me.   I know why you wan - na hate me.

Gtr. 3
(dist.)

Riff C   **End Riff C**

f

Gtr. 3: w/ Riff C (3 times)

I know why you wan - na hate me. 'Cause hate is all the world has ev - en seen late - ly.

Gtr. 4 (dist.): w/ Riff C (2 times)

I know why you wan - na hate me.   I know why you wan - na hate me.

Now I know why you wan - na hate me. 'Cause hate is all the world's ev - en seen late - ly.

And now you wan-na hate me 'cause

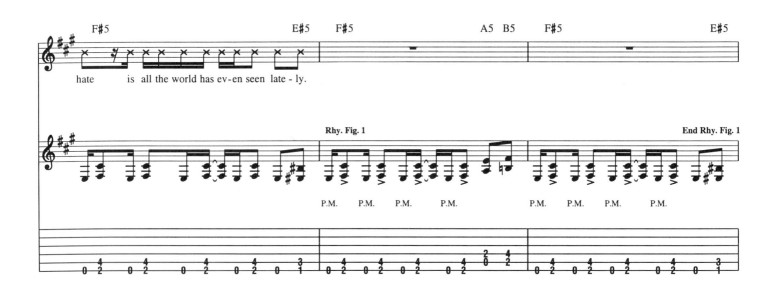

hate is all the world has ev-en seen late - ly.

And now you wan - na hate me 'cause hate is all the world has ev - en seen late - ly.

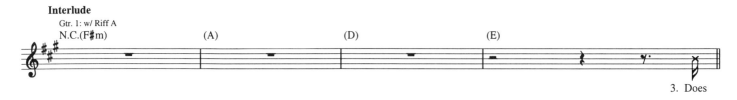

Interlude

3. Does

Tyler's Song

Lyrics by B. Dez Fafara

Music by Miguel Rascon, Rayna Foss-Rose, Mike Cox and B. Dez Fafara

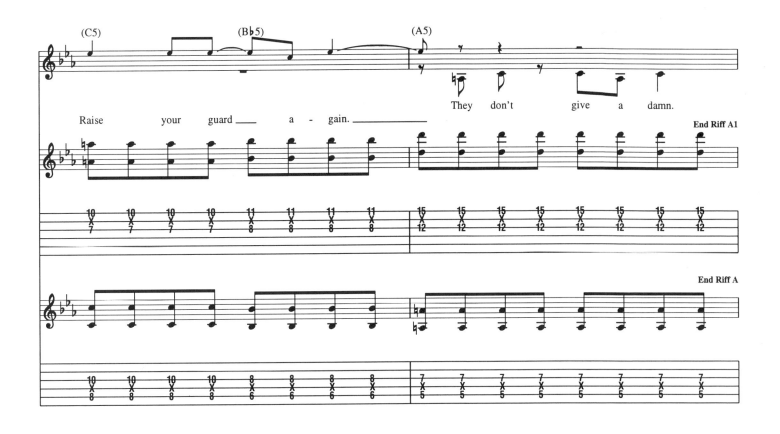

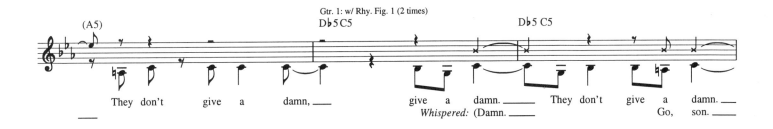

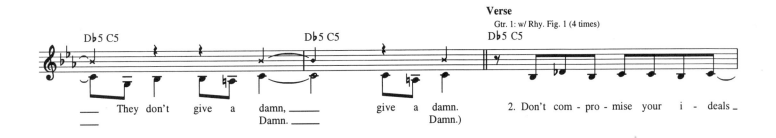

When I say to you, "Dad - dy loves you," un - der - stand I'm out in the real __

Chorus

Gtrs. 1 & 2: w/ Riffs A & A1 (2 times)

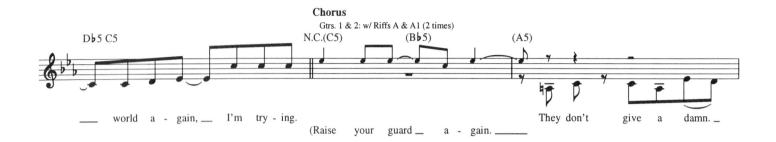

__ world a - gain, __ I'm try - ing.

(Raise your guard __ a - gain. __

They don't give a damn. __

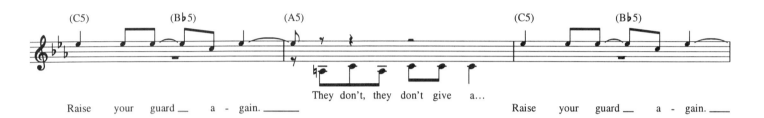

Raise your guard __ a - gain. __

They don't, they don't give a...

Raise your guard __ a - gain. __

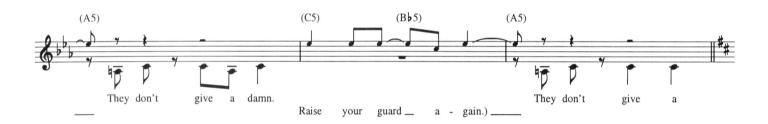

__ They don't give a damn.

Raise your guard __ a - gain.) __

They don't give a

Interlude

N.C.(B5)   (C5)

Bridge

Gtr. 1 tacet

N.C.(Bm)

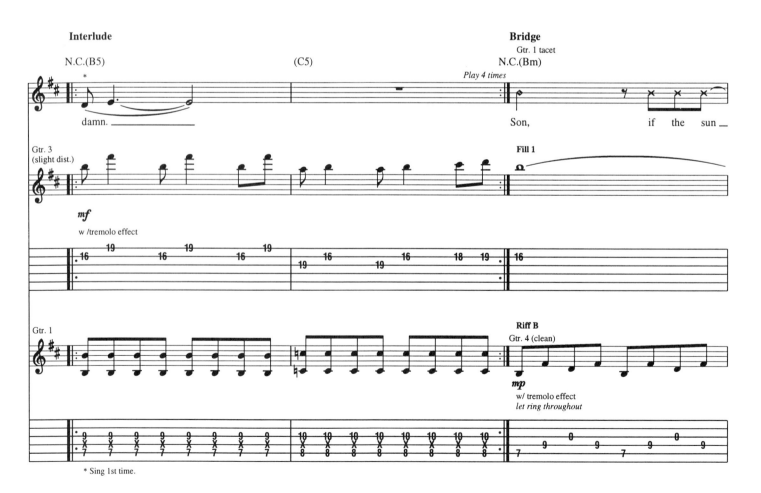

damn. __

Son,   if the sun __

Gtr. 3
(slight dist.)

Fill 1

mf
w/ tremolo effect

Gtr. 1

Riff B
Gtr. 4 (clean)

mp
w/ tremolo effect
let ring throughout

* Sing 1st time.

When Worlds Collide

Lyrics by Spider

Music by Powerman 5000

Tune down 1/2 step:
(low to high) Eb-Ab-Db-Gb-Bb-Eb

Intro

Moderately fast Rock ♩ = 145

Now this is what it's like when worlds col - lide. __ Now this is what it's like. __

Now this is what it's like. __ 1. What is it real - ly that's go - in' on here?

You've got the sys - tem for to - tal con - trol. Now is there an - y - bod - y out there?

Now watch us suf - fer, yeah, 'cause we can't go. __ What is it real - ly that is in your head?

* Synth. arr. for gtr.

Riff A

End Riff A

Gtr. 1: w/ Riff A (2 times)

Db(b5)   N.C.

** Gtr. 2 (dist.)

** Two gtrs. arr. for one.

Gtr. 4: w/ Fill 1

G5   F5 G5 F5 G5   F5 G5 F5 G5   F5 G5 F5 G5   F5 G5 B♭5

Are you go-ing with me? 'Cause I'm go-ing with you. That's the end of all ti - ime. _____

End Rhy. Fig. 1

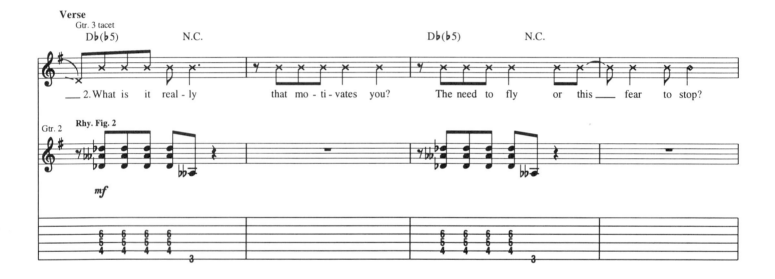

Verse
Gtr. 3 tacet
D♭(♭5)   N.C.   D♭(♭5)   N.C.

2. What is it real-ly that mo-ti-vates you? The need to fly or this ___ fear to stop?

Gtr. 2   **Rhy. Fig. 2**

mf

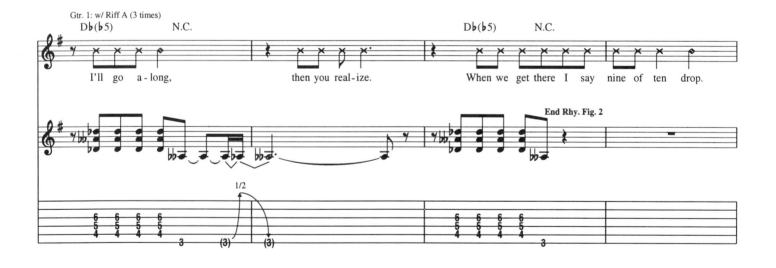

Gtr. 1: w/ Riff A (3 times)
D♭(♭5)   N.C.   D♭(♭5)   N.C.

I'll go a-long, then you real-ize. When we get there I say nine of ten drop.

End Rhy. Fig. 2

1/2

Gtr. 2: w/ Rhy. Fig. 2
D♭(♭5)   N.C.   D♭(♭5)   N.C.

Now who's the light and who is the dev-il? You can't de-cide so I'll be your guide.